Lakewood Memorial Library

IN MEMORY OF

Southwestern Central High
School, Lakewood Branch
Class of 1950

PRESENTED BY

John L. Hendrickson

North American
Historical Atlases

THE

COLONIES

A 1731 picture of the town of Boston as viewed from the sea.

North American
Historical Atlases

THE
COLONIES

Rebecca Stefoff

BENCHMARK BOOKS

MARSHALL CAVENDISH
NEW YORK

Benchmark Books
Marshall Cavendish Corporation
99 White Plains Road
Tarrytown, New York 10591

● ● ●

Library of Congress Cataloging-in-Publication Data
Stefoff, Rebecca, date.
The Colonies/Rebecca Stefoff
p. cm—(North American Historical Atlases)
Includes bibliographical references and index.
Summary: Discusses the establishment of European settlements and colonies in North
America during the 1600s, the growth of slavery, and relations with Indians.
ISBN 0-7614-1057-0 (lib.bdg.)
1. United States—History—Colonial period, ca. 1600–1775—Juvenile literature.   2. United States—History—Colonial period,
ca. 1600–1775—Maps—Juvenile Literature.   [1. United States—History—Colonial period, ca 1600–1775.]   I. Title.
E188 .S84   2001   99-047939   973.2—dc21

● ● ●

Printed in Hong Kong
1 3 5 7 8 6 4 2

● ● ●

Book Designer: Judith Turziano
Photo Researcher: Matthew Dudley

● ● ●

CREDITS
Front cover: *Art Resource*—Map of North America, late 17th c.
Back cover: *Virginia Museum of Fine Arts, Richmond. The Paul Mellon Collection.*
©*The Virginia Museum of Fine Arts*—Painting by John Gadsby Chapman (1808–1889),
Good Times in the New World (The Hope of Jamestown).

The photographs and maps in this book are used by permission and through the courtesy of:
Corbis-Bettmann: 2–3, 7, 8, 12, 13, 16, 17, 19, 20, 23, 24, 26, 28, 33, 38, 43.
The Library of Congress Maps Division: 9, 10, 14, 17, 25, 35, 36, 37.

Contents

Chapter One

EUROPEAN CLAIMS

Once explorers from Europe had reached the Americas, their nations promptly set about laying claim to the newfound lands—and a big part of claiming a territory was setting up a **colony**. Spain, France, England, and the Netherlands planted settlements that grew into great European empires in North America.

Europeans like this missionary, shown preaching in the forest with a Bible in his hand, thought their religion was superior to all others. They were determined to make the Native Americans into Christians.

The Spanish Borderlands

The first Europeans to establish permanent colonies in what is now the United States were the Spanish. By the mid-1500s they had conquered most of the Caribbean Islands and Mexico, which they called New Spain.

In 1565 the Spanish built a fort on the east coast of Florida. This outpost became St. Augustine, the oldest city in the United States. The old fort still stands, a reminder of the fact that Spain owned Florida for hundreds of years. Then, to keep other European powers from settling on the doorstep of New Spain, Spanish authorities in that colony sent soldiers, **missionaries**, and colonists north into the deserts and mountains of the Southwest. In 1598 Juan de Oñate led 129 soldiers and their families into New Mexico. Despite near-starvation and quarrels among the soldiers, the little colony survived. In 1610 it became the town of Santa Fe, New Mexico.

In the late 1600s the Spanish began colonizing Texas and Arizona. They built three kinds of settlements. *Presidios* (preh SEE dee ohs) were military forts. *Pueblos* (PWEH blohs), or towns, were centers of trade. Missions were communities run by religious brotherhoods. Most included churches, small towns, and farmland. Spanish soldiers forced the local Indians to work on the missions, while the **monks** set about converting them to Christianity.

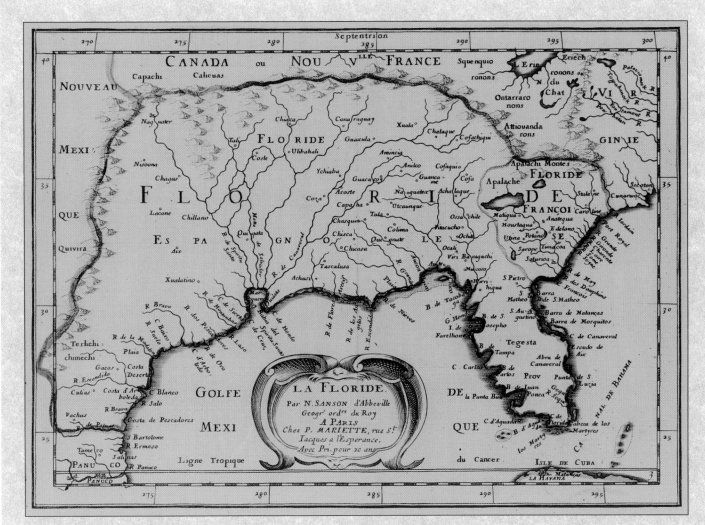

French mapmaker Nicholas Sanson's 1657 image of part of North America is not very accurate—notice how close Lake Erie, in the upper right, is to Florida. The map shows North America divided between French and Spanish territory and does not indicate the small new English colonies on the Atlantic coast.

In 1769 a monk named Junípero Serra founded a mission at San Diego, California. Now Spain claimed Florida, Texas, New Mexico, Arizona, and California. These were the Spanish Borderlands—the wild, rugged, and thinly inhabited frontier of New Spain.

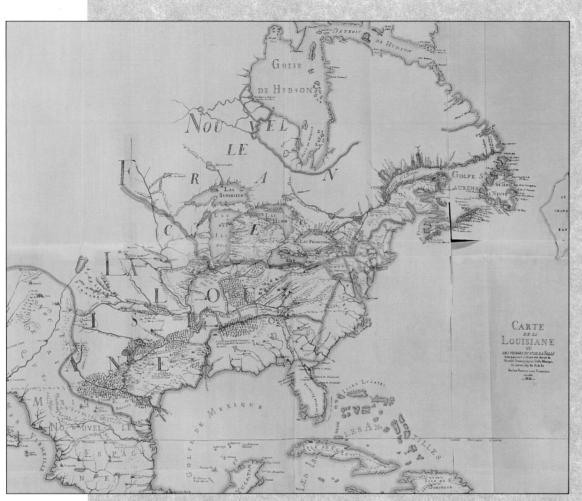

The French North American territories of Nouvelle France (Canada) and La Louisiane (Louisiana) overshadow other countries' territories in this French map. Colonial maps did more than record geography— they fed national pride and supported territorial claims.

to come were fishermen, who merely visited during the summer months. In the late 1500s the French tried several times to establish settlements, but each attempt failed after a few years. Then Samuel de Champlain spent five years exploring the Atlantic coast, looking for the perfect spot. In 1608 he decided on Quebec, on the St. Lawrence River, and France founded its first permanent North American colony. Over the next 100 years Quebec became the center of government, trade, and culture for the large colony called New France.

The St. Lawrence River was France's highway into Canada. Champlain spent years exploring it and the Great Lakes to which

The French in Canada

While the Spanish were staking their claim to the southern part of North America, the French moved into Canada in the north. First it led. Fur trappers and traders called *coureurs de bois* (coo RUHR deh bwah), "woods-runners," also pushed west toward the heart of the continent. Boatmen called *voyageurs* (voy ah ZHUR)

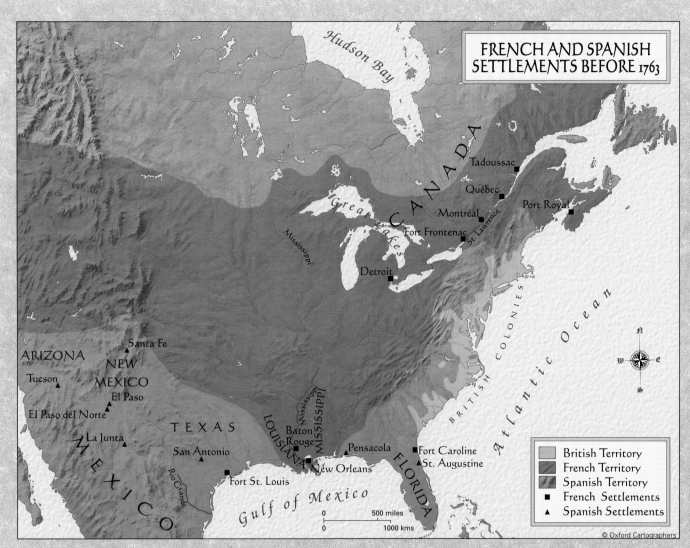

Hudson Bay

C A N A D A

Great Lakes

Tadoussac

Québec

Montréal

Port Royal

Fort Frontenac

St. Lawrence

Mississippi

Detroit

B R I T I S H   C O L O N I E S

A t l a n t i c   O c e a n

ARIZONA

Santa Fe

NEW
MEXICO

Tucson

El Paso

El Paso del Norte

La Junta

T E X A S

LOUISIANA

Mississippi

MISSISSIPPI

M E X I C O

San Antonio

Baton
Rouge

Pensacola

Fort Caroline

St. Augustine

New Orleans

FLORIDA

Rio Grande

Fort St. Louis

Gulf of Mexico

0   500 miles

0   1000 kms

© Oxford Cartographers

	British Territory
	French Territory
	Spanish Territory
■	French Settlements
▲	Spanish Settlements

Spain moved into North America from the south, sending expeditions of exploration and conquest
out from its footholds on the Caribbean islands and in Mexico. France entered the continent from two
directions. In the northeast the St. Lawrence River and the Great Lakes provided a waterway for French
travelers who mastered the use of the Native American canoe, while in the south a colony founded
near the mouth of the Mississippi River became the basis for a vast territorial claim. Yet France
never sent enough colonists to establish strong control over the land it claimed.

THE PERFECT FUR

 Fashions change quickly these days, but between 1650 and 1850 one item remained in style and in demand—fur. Men's hats and coats made of warm, waterproof beaver fur were highly prized all over Europe. The fur could be removed from the skin and pressed together to form a heavy cloth called felt, ideal for hatmaking, or whole beaver **pelts** could be made into capes and coats.

By the 1500s the beavers of Europe had been hunted into extinction. But when early explorers and settlers discovered that the streams and ponds of North America teemed with the plump, glossy creatures, the rush was on. In the early 1600s French, English, and Dutch merchants developed trade networks among the Native tribes, exchanging axes, needles, blankets, and other metal and cloth goods—as well as liquor—for furs. By the 1660s the fur trade had almost wiped out the beaver in Massachusetts, but the trade kept moving west along rivers and lakes. Much of the North American interior was first explored by people searching for furs.

American artist Frederic Remington immortalized the fur trapper in this 1890 image. By that time the fur trade was long dead, but the romance of the early trapper-explorers who had pioneered routes into Canada and the American West still lingered.

made long journeys in Indian-style canoes, carrying loads of valuable furs from the backcountry to Quebec.

Meanwhile, French explorers from Canada probed south along the Mississippi River toward the Gulf of Mexico. In 1699 they built a fort in Louisiana and claimed the surrounding territory. France founded the port of New

Orleans there in 1718. The French hoped that by controlling the Mississippi River valley they could keep both Spain and England from getting a foothold in the center of North America.

The English Colonies

Like France, England tried several times to establish North American colonies in the late 1500s and early 1600s—and failed each time. Then, in 1607, three ships sailed into Chesa-

This old woodcut of the settlers at Jamestown bluntly illustrates one of the colony's biggest problems—very few of the first settlers were willing or able to do anything useful. Most considered themselves too good for common labor, preferring to grumble and complain.

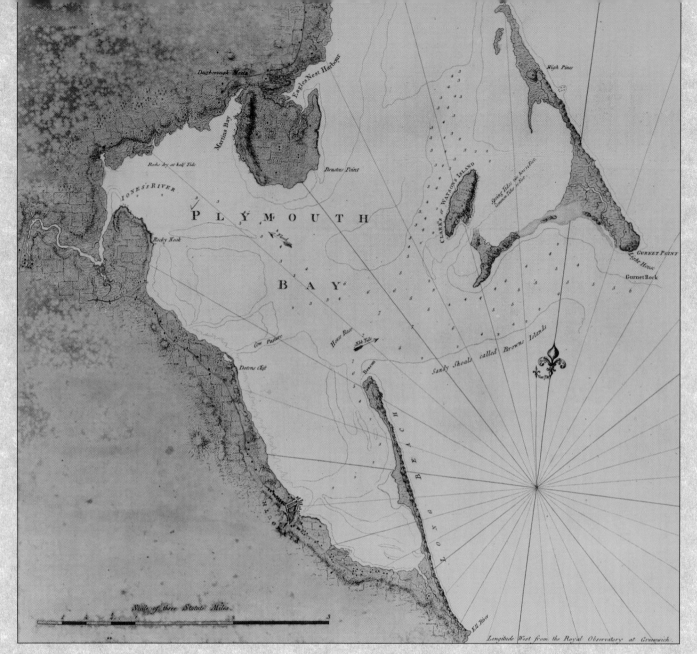

English investors formed the Plymouth Company to plant settlements on the American coast.
After an attempt to colonize Maine failed, they sent two ships toward Virginia in 1620. One ship
leaked and had to turn back to England. The other landed in America but missed Virginia.
That ship, the **Mayflower**, finally came ashore at a bay in Massachusetts. The colonists named
it Plymouth Bay and settled along the shoreline. The land was vacant because the local
Indians had recently died of diseases they caught from European explorers.

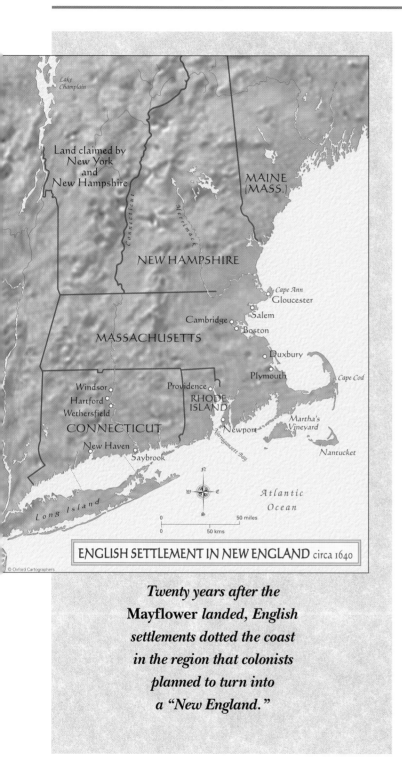

ENGLISH SETTLEMENT IN NEW ENGLAND circa 1640

Twenty years after the **Mayflower** *landed, English settlements dotted the coast in the region that colonists planned to turn into a "New England."*

peake Bay, Virginia. Aboard were 144 settlers sent by a company of English merchants. They founded a community they called Jamestown, named after the king of England.

Unlike earlier settlements, Jamestown survived—but just barely. The location had little good farmland and plenty of disease-carrying mosquitoes. It was surrounded by Native Americans who did not welcome the intruders. Worst of all, the settlers knew little about practical things such as farming and carpentry. Instead of working to survive, they spent a good deal of time arguing and searching for gold and silver (they didn't find any).

Many settlers died during the winter of 1609-1610, which they called "the starving time." But Jamestown endured, and in time new colonists arrived. In 1619 the company let the colonists form their own lawmaking body called the House of Burgesses. It didn't have much real power, but it was the beginning of America's tradition of self-government. The following year a ship called the *Mayflower* carried another batch of colonists to the Atlantic coast. They planned to land in Virginia but came ashore farther north, at a place called Plymouth in what is now Massachusetts. A second English colony took root there.

New Netherland

In 1609 an English captain named Henry Hudson sailed into New York Harbor and up

AFRICANS IN NORTH AMERICA

A Dutch ship landed at Jamestown in 1619 to unload a human cargo—twenty black Africans to work in the Virginia planters' fields. These were the first slaves brought to North American shores. But not all blacks in the early Virginia colony were slaves. Some black residents were free property owners. Starting in the 1660s, however, greater numbers of enslaved Africans were brought by force to Virginia, and soon slaves outnumbered free blacks. In the years to come, slavery would become established in many of the North American colonies. Both blacks and whites were part of America from the beginning—but not on equal terms.

The first black slaves brought to North America arrived in Jamestown on a Dutch ship.

the Hudson River. The Dutch had paid for his voyage, and they claimed the area he had explored. Merchants from the Netherlands set up forts and fur-trading posts along the river. In the 1620s a Dutch trading firm called the Dutch West Indies Company began bringing settlers to New Netherland, as the colony was called. Its main port and biggest town was New Amsterdam, at the southern tip of Manhattan Island. In 1626 the company bought the entire island from the local Native Americans.

New Amsterdam was a multicultural place. Half of its population was Dutch—farmers, traders, crafts workers, soldiers, merchants, and their families. The rest came from Sweden, Finland, Norway, England, Spain, Portugal, Italy, and other European countries. New Netherland also had Native Americans, free and enslaved Africans, and a community of European Jews. One resident wrote in 1642 that he could hear eighteen languages spoken in the colony.

Peter Stuyvesant arriving in New Amsterdam in 1647. Stuyvesant, who had lost a leg fighting the Portuguese in the West Indies, governed the Dutch colony with a heavy hand for nearly twenty years.

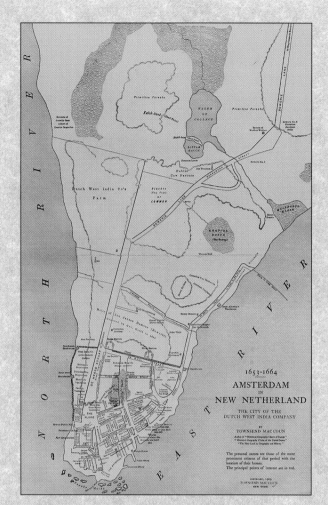

By 1664 The Dutch had turned the southern end of Manhattan Island into a bustling town. The protective wall across the north end of town marked what is still called Wall Street. North of it "primitive forests" covered what would one day be downtown New York City.

Chapter Two

NATIVE AMERICANS & SETTLERS

North America was not an empty place waiting for Europeans to fill it. The colonists who came to North America had to deal with its original inhabitants, the Native Americans. The two races formed many kinds of relationships, some friendly, some not. But whether the Europeans killed the Native Americans, converted them, traded with them, or simply drove them away, one thing was almost always true—they did not treat them as equals.

Early Contacts

About four and a half million Native Americans lived north of Mexico when the Europeans began colonizing North America. These Indians lived throughout the continent in a wide variety of different nations, or tribes, each with its own language, customs, culture, and way of living off the land.

Most of the early settlers had encounters with the Native Americans. In fact, the Indians themselves were one of the reasons why both Spain and France were interested in North America. These nations believed that it was important to convert the Indians to the Roman Catholic faith, and they went to great efforts to do so, although their methods differed.

In the Southwest, Spanish monks and soldiers did not always give the Indians a choice—Native Americans were forced to live in missions and punished if they continued to practice their own religions. They also had to farm and perform other services for the white colonists. As soon as Oñate and his followers arrived in New Mexico, for example, they forced the Pueblo Indians to accept them as masters. One Spanish monk wrote that the men who colonized the Borderlands were "enemies of all sorts of work" who made the Indians work for them.

Londoners were charmed by Pocahontas, the chieftain's daughter who married a colonist and visited England with him. Sadly, their interest in one Native American woman did not result in better long-term relations with her people.

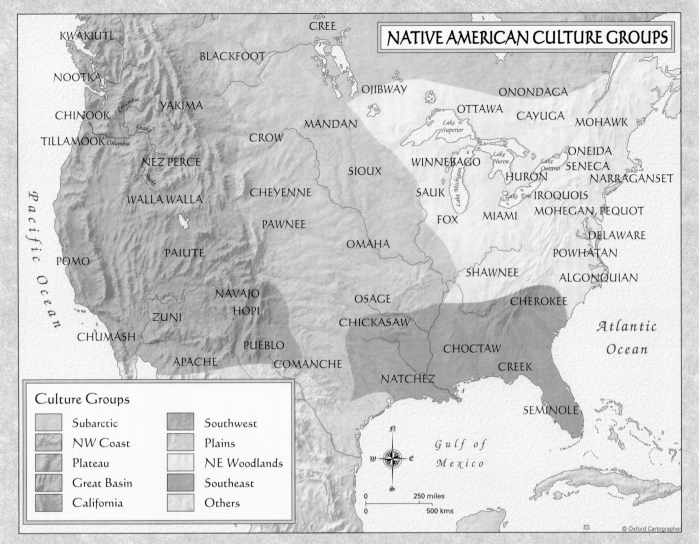

NATIVE AMERICAN CULTURE GROUPS

CREE
KWAKIUTL
BLACKFOOT
NOOTKA
OJIBWAY
ONONDAGA
OTTAWA CAYUGA
YAKIMA
CHINOOK
MANDAN
MOHAWK
TILLAMOOK
Columbia
CROW
ONEIDA
NEZ PERCE
WINNEBAGO
SENECA
SIOUX
HURON
NARRAGANSET
WALLA WALLA
CHEYENNE
SAUK
IROQUOIS
PAWNEE
FOX MIAMI
MOHEGAN, PEQUOT
OMAHA
DELAWARE
POMO
PAIUTE
POWHATAN
SHAWNEE
ALGONQUIAN
NAVAJO
OSAGE
CHEROKEE
ZUNI HOPI
CHICKASAW
Atlantic
CHUMASH
Ocean
PUEBLO
CHOCTAW
APACHE
COMANCHE
CREEK
NATCHEZ
SEMINOLE

Pacific Ocean

Gulf of Mexico

Culture Groups

Subarctic	Southwest
NW Coast	Plains
Plateau	NE Woodlands
Great Basin	Southeast
California	Others

0   250 miles
0   500 kms

© Oxford Cartographer

The European colonists encountered hundreds of Native American peoples belonging to ten large families, or culture groups. The homelands of the major nations, or tribes, are shown here as they appeared before the arrival of the Europeans altered settlement patterns and drove many Native Americans into new regions.

The French, in general, treated the Native Americans more kindly, often living with them and learning their languages. Many of the "black robes," as the Indians called French priests and monks, showed respect for Indian culture. And French-Canadian trappers and traders often married Indian women and spent years living among the Indians.

The English colonists at Jamestown had the Powhatan Indians for neighbors. Although the Indians gave the starving colonists some corn, relations between the two races were not always

The English who settled along the Atlantic coast and the French who entered Canada along the St. Lawrence River interacted with these Native American groups. By the late 1670s most of the Native Americans in the English colonies had either died, fled north to French Canada or west into the unsettled interior, or been forced into communities set aside for them—the first Indian reservations. The French were more successful at building lasting relationships with the Native Americans. Because far fewer French colonists than English ones came to North America, the French felt less pressure to drive the Native Americans off the land.

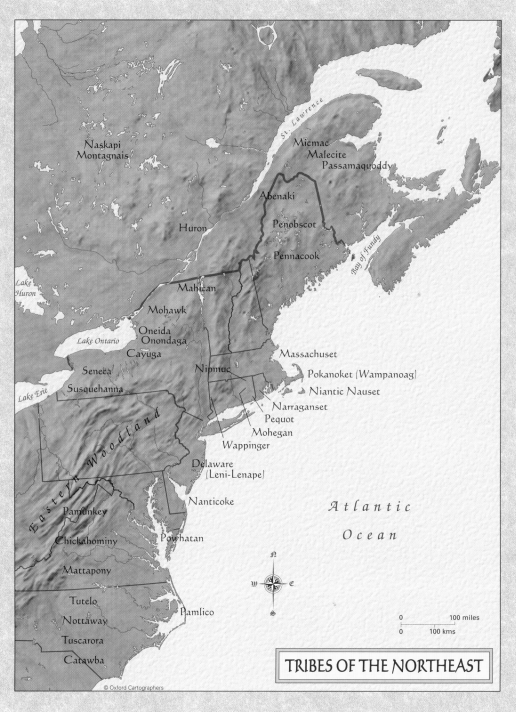

TRIBES OF THE NORTHEAST

TOBACCO

Even before settlement began at Jamestown, Europeans knew of a plant that the Native Americans smoked in pipes to seal agreements, celebrate religious festivals, and mark important occasions such as meetings of elders. That plant was tobacco, and the Indians offered it to the European visitors. Most Europeans found tobacco harsh and unpleasant. For a time it almost seemed that the habit of smoking might not catch on. Then, in 1614, John Rolfe of Jamestown experimented with tobacco seeds from the Caribbean islands and produced a variety that Europeans found enjoyable. Tobacco saved the Jamestown colony, which exported 2,300 pounds (1,045 kilograms) of dried tobacco in 1616 and more than a hundred times as much ten years later. "All our riches for the present do consist in Tobacco," wrote one early colonist-planter. The weed has been a profitable crop for the American Southeast ever since then.

The tobacco plant was one of many American products that found an eager market in Europe. King James I of England, however, had more insight than the new tobacco consumers—he called smoking a "vile and stinking" custom.

friendly. In 1614, however, matters improved when colonist John Rolfe married Pocahontas, the daughter of the local chieftain. At Plymouth several Native Americans befriended the settlers. One of them, Squanto, showed the colonists how to grow American crops such as corn and pumpkins and where to fish and hunt. He also helped them make a treaty with the local Wampanoag tribe. Without his help, Plymouth might have ended up as another failure.

Living Together

The meeting of Europeans and Native Americans affected both peoples. One effect was that the Europeans brought new diseases to the Americans—illnesses such as measles, influenza, and smallpox to which the Indians had no resistance. **Epidemics** swept through the Americas. During the first 150 years of colonization, more Indians died from European diseases than from any other cause.

When Europeans and Indians met, the two sides generally exchanged gifts. The Europeans welcomed food and furs, while the

The American holiday, Thanksgiving, is traditionally celebrated with turkey and pumpkins, the foods the Native Americans gave to the starving New England colonists in November of 1621.

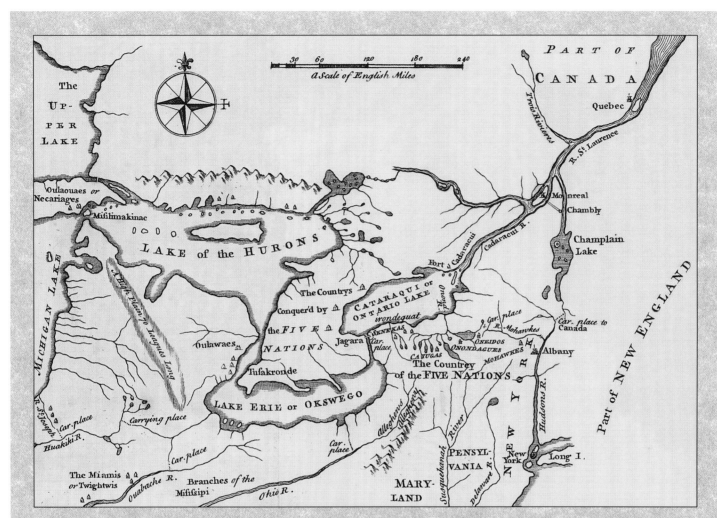

An English map shows New York's Five Nations, the most serious Native American threat to the English colonies. The northwestern frontier as far as Lake Superior ("The Upper Lake") is illustrated, with special attention to canoe routes. "Carrying place" or "Car. place" shows where a traveler would have to portage, hauling his canoe overland between two bodies of water.

Indians quickly came to prize such unfamiliar goods as glass, steel, and woolen cloth. This exchange grew into a large-scale trade that dramatically changed the Native American economy. Some Indian communities stopped producing food for themselves, instead working to get furs and hides for the whites. They became dependent on food and other supplies they bought from the whites and many tribes began trading manufactured European goods among themselves.

Of all trade goods, the Indians valued guns and ammunition most highly. The Europeans and their firearms changed the balance of power among the tribes, giving a huge advantage to those who acquired guns from their white trading partners. After the Dutch supplied guns to the Mohawk Indians, for example, the Mohawk terrorized Montagnais and Algonquian communities in northern New Netherland.

At the same time, Indians became involved in the rivalry among the European powers in North America. Some tribes formed **alliances** with the Dutch and English, others with the French. The Abenaki people who lived along the Maine coast were allies of the French, and together the French and Abenaki drove English settlers out of the region in the late 1600s. One of the most powerful Native American groups of the early colonial period was the Five Nations of northern New York, sometimes called the Iroquois Confederacy. It consisted of the Onondaga, Mohawk, Seneca, Cayuga, and Oneida tribes. As allies of the Dutch and later the English, the Iroquois frequently attacked the French in Canada and Indian allies of the French.

Conflicts Over Land

It didn't take the Native Americans long to realize that the Europeans were not just visitors and occasional trading partners. They were coming to stay—and in ever-increasing numbers. This was especially true in the English colonies, which attracted many more settlers than the French or Spanish colonies. Almost

The arrival of the Europeans tilted the political balance that existed among Native American groups, many of whom had been in conflict before the Europeans came. Some Native Americans found that alliances with the well-armed Europeans gave them an edge over their traditional enemies. Several New England tribes, for example, joined the English in a war against the large and powerful Pequot tribe. The allies set the main Pequot village on fire and then slaughtered the villagers as they fled.

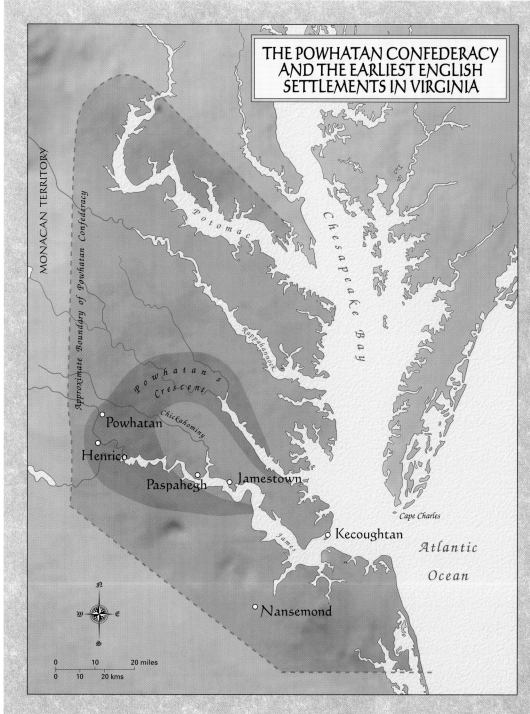

THE POWHATAN CONFEDERACY AND THE EARLIEST ENGLISH SETTLEMENTS IN VIRGINIA

MONACAN TERRITORY

Approximate Boundary of Powhatan Confederacy

Potomac

Rappahannock

Powhatan's Crescent

Chickahominy

Chesapeake Bay

Powhatan

Henrico

Paspahegh

Jamestown

James

Kecoughtan

Cape Charles

Nansemond

Atlantic Ocean

0   10   20 miles
0   10   20 kms

The forceful Native American leader Powhatan formed a confederacy—a loose association of villages under his rule—around the Chesapeake Bay during the early 1600s, when English settlers were arriving. Relations between the colonists and the confederacy began in uneasy peace but descended into prolonged fighting.

The colonists took pains to befriend chieftains whom they considered to have royal status. Here they are shown "crowning" Powhatan, who had managed to dominate a number of local Native American groups.

overnight the landscape around Jamestown, Plymouth, and other settlements changed from forest to fields and towns. As more settlers arrived, they took more land.

The Indians were not willing to hand over their traditional homelands, or to see them permanently occupied by large numbers of Europeans. Wars soon broke out. The Powhatan Indians and the Jamestown colonists fought in the 1620s. In 1637 the Plymouth colonists and their allies, the Narragansett Indians, wiped out the Pequot tribe. One of the biggest conflicts took place in Massachusetts in 1675 when Indians united under a Wampanoag leader named Metacomet but called King Philip by the whites. King Philip's War ended with a settlers' victory that broke the strength of the local tribes for good. But warfare between colonists and Indians—almost always over the basic question of who controlled the land—would continue elsewhere for years.

Conflict was not limited to the English colonies. The Pueblo Revolt caught fire in the Spanish colony of New Mexico in 1680 after priests and officials punished the Pueblo Indians for practicing their old religion. The Indians rose against the Spanish, killing some and driving the rest away, and remained in control of New Mexico until Spanish troops retook it fifteen years later. In Louisiana, when fighting broke out between the French colonists and the Natchez Indians, the French found allies among the Choctaw Indians and wiped out the Natchez.

A Changing Population

Warfare, epidemics, and the arrival of shipload after shipload of Europeans changed the population of North America during the 1600s. In New England alone the number of Native Americans dropped from 100,000 in 1600 to 10,000 in 1675. Of the million or so Indians who had lived east of the Mississippi River before the English landed at Jamestown, only about 150,000 remained in the mid-1700s. Some tribes,

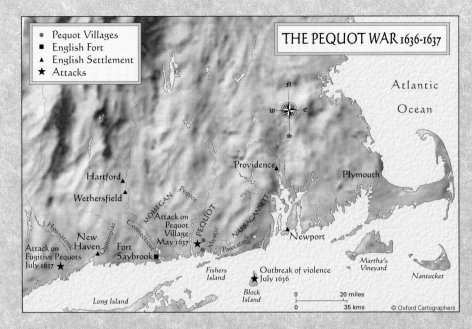

THE PEQUOT WAR 1636-1637

- ● Pequot Villages
- ■ English Fort
- ▲ English Settlement
- ★ Attacks

Atlantic Ocean

Hartford
Wethersfield
Providence
Plymouth
MOHEGAN
Pequot
Attack on
Pequot
Village
May 1637
PEQUOT
NARRAGANSETT
Housatonic
New Haven
Quinnipiac
Connecticut
Fort Saybrook
Mystic
Pawcatuck
Newport
Attack on
Fugitive Pequots
July 1637
Fishers Island
Outbreak of violence
July 1636
Martha's Vineyard
Nantucket
Long Island
Block Island

0   20 miles
0   35 kms

© Oxford Cartographers

The Pequots occupied a stretch of coastline that the English colonists were eager to control. In addition, other local Native American groups were displeased with the growing wealth and power of the Pequots, who prospered because they were trading partners with the Dutch colony of New Netherland. These groups joined forces with colonists from Connecticut and Massachusetts to crush the Pequots.

San Juan
HOPI
APACHE
Taos
Picuris
Tesuque
Santa Fe
August 1680
Pecos
NAVAJO
ZUÑI
Zia
Rio Grande
Little Colorado
Albuquerque
Zuni
Acoma
Pecos

● Indian Villages
▲ Spanish Settlements
★ Battles

Bac
San Pedro
APACHE
COMANCHE
PIMA
El Paso
MEXICO

© Oxford Cartographers

THE PUEBLO REVOLT 1680

0   70 miles
0   120 kms

The Pueblo Revolt was the most serious outbreak of Native American resistance in the Spanish borderlands during the long history of colonial settlement there. It turned a population of 25,000 to 30,000 Indians against fewer than 2,400 settlers. The Indians were less interested in killing the Spanish than in driving them out of their land. They succeeded in forcing the Spanish to retreat south to El Paso, although the retreat was only temporary. The Spanish eventually reconquered the area, but they had learned a lesson. They never again outlawed the traditional religious practices of the Native Americans who lived there.

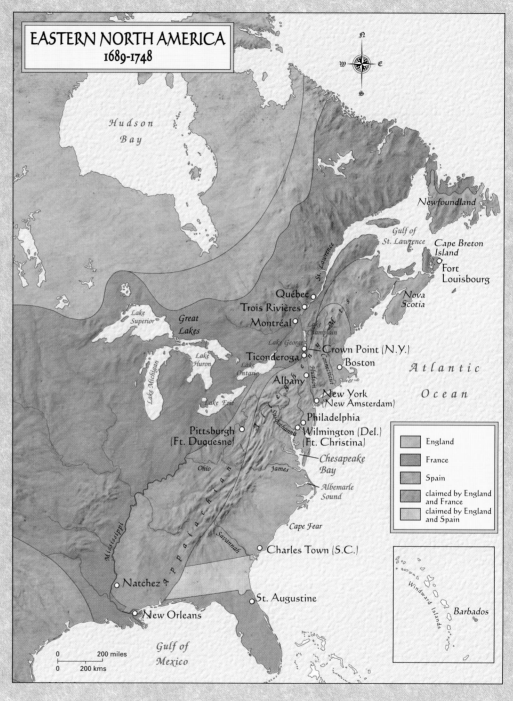

EASTERN NORTH AMERICA
1689-1748

Hudson
Bay

Newfoundland

Gulf of
St. Lawrence

Cape Breton
Island

Fort
Louisbourg

Québec

Trois Rivières

Montréal

Nova
Scotia

Lake
Superior

Great
Lakes

Lake
Champlain

Lake George

Crown Point (N.Y.)

Ticonderoga

Boston

Lake
Huron

Lake Ontario

Albany

Atlantic

Lake Michigan

Lake Erie

Hudson

Connecticut

New York
(New Amsterdam)

Ocean

Philadelphia

Pittsburgh
(Ft. Duquesne)

Susquehanna

Wilmington (Del.)
(Ft. Christina)

Chesapeake
Bay

Ohio

James

Appalachian

Albemarle
Sound

Mississippi

Savannah

Cape Fear

Charles Town (S.C.)

Natchez

St. Augustine

New Orleans

Gulf of
Mexico

England

France

Spain

claimed by England
and France

claimed by England
and Spain

Windward Islands

Barbados

0   200 miles
0   200 kms

The European nations often disagreed and sometimes went to war over the boundaries of their claims in North America. Land changed hands as the result of treaties made in far-off European capitals. The island of Nova Scotia, for example, passed between the English and the French several times.

RUSSIANS IN ALASKA

Long after the Spanish, French, Dutch, and English had begun to colonize southern and eastern North America, the northwest corner of the continent remained unknown and mysterious. The first white people to arrive there did not come across the Atlantic, like other European explorers. They came across the Pacific, from Russia.

Vitus Bering, a Danish captain hired by Russia, sailed to the Aleutian Islands and the coast of Alaska in 1741. The Russians took home the soft, silky pelts of more than 1,500 sea otters. At once other Russians set out for the fur-rich "eastern islands." The Russians brought the Aleutians and then Alaska's southeastern coast under their control by attacking and enslaving the Native Americans who lived there. Although some Indians fought back fiercely, by 1799 two-thirds of them were dead. The Russians built a permanent capital at Sitka and controlled Alaska until 1867. The Russian heritage of religion, architecture, and customs is still seen in some parts of Alaska today.

such as the Pequot, had all but disappeared.

At the same time, the number of European settlers in eastern North America kept rising. So did the number of African Americans. By 1680 the population of the English colonies included 143,000 whites and nearly 7,000 blacks. By 1780 it would reach 2,157,000 whites and 569,000 blacks.

Chapter Three

THE THIRTEEN COLONIES

ngland's first few settlements along the Atlantic coast became a string of thirteen colonies between French Canada in the north and Spanish Florida in the south. The English colonies differed from those of Spain and France. They were closer to Europe, they had a European-style climate, and they welcomed people from many countries. As a result the English colonies attracted far more settlers than New Spain or New France. Some came for religious freedom, some to escape debt or prison. Some sought jobs, land, or wealth through trade. And some were brought by force. Together they created a multicultural, thriving, fast-growing society.

New England

The northernmost cluster of English colonies came to be known as New England. The first to become established was Massachusetts, founded by several groups seeking religious freedom. The **Pilgrims** landed at Plymouth in 1620, and ten years later the **Puritans** founded the Massachusetts Bay Colony, with its capital at Boston. At that time Massachusetts included what is now Maine.

In 1636 two groups left the Massachusetts Bay Colony to start new settlements where they could practice their own versions of Puritan Christianity. Attracted by fertile soil and good trade prospects, one group settled along the Connecticut River. The other settled in a small region east of Connecticut and south of Massachusetts. Known as Rhode Island, this colony was the first to welcome people of all religions.

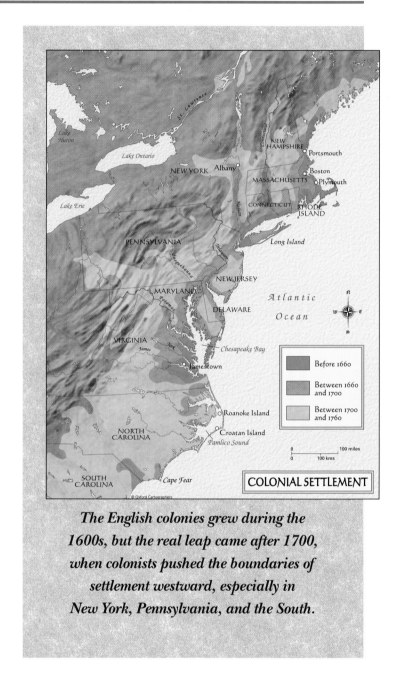

The English colonies grew during the 1600s, but the real leap came after 1700, when colonists pushed the boundaries of settlement westward, especially in New York, Pennsylvania, and the South.

Herman Moll, a Dutch mapmaker working in England, made this map of New England and
the Middle Atlantic colonies in the 1730s. One of the most accurate maps of its time, it shows the many
roads, trails, towns, and villages that had sprung up in this industrious part of the colonies.

The English may have settled the Middle Atlantic coast, but other nations remained interested in the region. This French map of the Chesapeake and the surrounding country shows how both Native American villages and English communities were clustered along waterways.

England was not ideal for farming. But it had plenty of useful timber to support a shipbuilding industry, and it also had many excellent ports to house fleets of trade, fishing, and whaling vessels. New England became the seafaring center of the colonies.

Middle Atlantic Colonies

The Dutch and Swedes were the first to settle the land between Massachusetts and Jamestown. The Dutch founded New Netherland in the 1620s, and in the 1630s Sweden claimed and occupied several settlements along the Delaware River. In 1664 the Dutch surrendered New Netherland to an English fleet, and the English took over the colony, which they renamed New York. The Duke of York, the colony's new owner, gave the southern part of it to two English noblemen. They named their colony New Jersey and began renting out pieces of it to settlers. In 1702 New Jersey

Other groups moved into the northern part of the Massachusetts colony. Some sought religious freedom, and some hoped to make a living fishing on the coast or trading for furs inland. In 1679 this region became a separate colony called New Hampshire.

Hilly, heavily forested, and thin-soiled, New

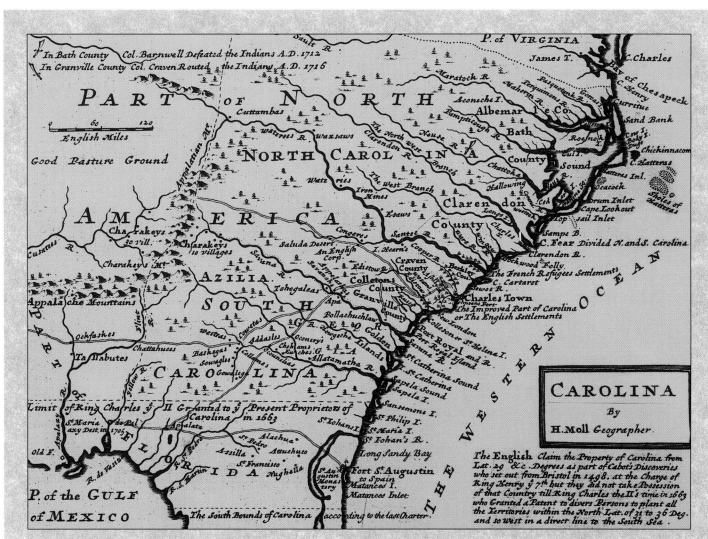

Moll's map of Carolina spans the area between southern Virginia and northern Florida, with Georgia included in South Carolina. Symbols resembling swords mark the sites of military victories over Native Americans. Note the attention given to north Florida—many English subjects were already eager to take it from Spain.

passed into the control of the king of England.

Just west of New Jersey was Pennsylvania, founded in 1681 by William Penn on land given him by the king to repay a debt. Penn had two reasons for establishing the colony. He hoped to make money from settlers' rents, and he wanted to create a place where members of his faith—a Protestant group called the Society of Friends, sometimes known as Quakers—could freely follow their beliefs. For this reason Penn called his colony a "holy experiment." It included the former Swedish settlements. Later, part of southern Pennsylvania split off to form a separate colony called Delaware.

The Middle Atlantic colonies had fertile soil and a good climate for farming. Agriculture flourished, and after farmers began sending their wheat and livestock to New York and Philadelphia to be shipped to overseas buyers, these ports grew into the largest cities in the English colonies. By 1770 Philadelphia's population was 28,000 and New York's was 25,000. The middle colonies were also noted for crafts workshops and the beginnings of American industry—New Jersey, for example, had the colonies' biggest iron mill.

Southern Colonies

Virginia, the first of the southern colonies, was founded by a trading company that hoped to make a profit. George Calvert, Lord Baltimore, founded the Maryland colony in 1632 in the hope of making his fortune in the tobacco trade, but he also wanted to establish a safe home for English Catholics, who were highly unpopular in England.

The eight English noblemen who founded Carolina in 1663 had no high ideals. They sim-

Cecil Calvert, the second Lord Baltimore, was the true founder of the Maryland colony (his father had planned the colony but died before settlement could begin). Here Cecil Calvert and his young daughter brandish a map of the Chesapeake Bay while an African slave looks on. Maryland, like other tobacco-growing states, would depend heavily upon slave labor.

ply wanted to use the colony that the king had given them to make money through trade and by selling and renting land to settlers. Tension between plantation owners in the south and small farmers in the north caused a split, and in 1729 the colony broke into North Carolina and South Carolina.

Georgia was the southernmost of the thirteen colonies and the last to be founded. It was created in 1733 as a home for Protestants and a place where poor people and **debtors** could improve their lot in life by working on their own small farms. But the British government did not make Georgia available for these uses simply out of kindness. Often at war with Spain, Britain wanted to build a barrier of English settlers between Spanish Florida and the prosperous plantation colonies to the north.

From the start, the southern colonies were given over to agriculture. Large plantations and small farms alike produced cash crops—products to be exported rather than used locally. The chief crops of the region were tobacco, rice, and **indigo**, although the south also exported timber and cattle and deer hides. The cash-crop economy required a great deal of labor in fields and processing sheds, and planters turned to slavery to provide that labor. Eventually the southern colonies had the largest black population in British North America.

Who Came to America?

Most of those who came to the English North American colonies in the 1600s were from the British Isles. Of the 400,000 people who left Britain for the colonies during the century, the majority were English, although some were Scottish, Irish, or Welsh. More than half of them went to the British island colonies in the Caribbean. A third went to the southern mainland colonies, especially Virginia and Maryland, and about a tenth went to New England and the Middle Atlantic colonies.

The flow of newcomers changed during the 1700s. Scottish and Irish **immigrants** outnumbered English ones. In addition, about 100,000 Germans and several thousand French Protestants arrived in the British colonies. But only a fifth of all immigrants settled in the Caribbean colonies. The mainland now attracted the great majority of settlers.

A World of Trade

The North American colonies did not exist on their own, cut off from the rest of the world. England intended them to serve a role in the large-scale trade that was beginning to weave together all parts of the globe. The colonies' role was to export raw materials to England and to import finished goods that had been manufactured in English workshops and factories.

Philadelphia, New York, and New England ports such as Boston were the colonies' centers of trade and commerce. From them ships carried cargoes of timber, wheat, furs, rice, and other products to English ports, returning with loads of clothing, furniture, metal-and glassware, paper, and other goods. The North American colonies also traded with the Caribbean colonies, exchanging flour, fish, and meat for cash, sugar, **molasses**, and slaves. Trade routes formed a triangle between England, the Caribbean, and the North American colonies.

The growth of slavery led to another triangular trade pattern. Colonial ships carried **rum**, iron tools, cloth, and other goods to West Africa to be traded for slaves. On the second leg of the triangle, the "Middle Passage," they carried the slaves to the Caribbean. On the third leg they carried slaves, gold, molasses, and sugar to New England. There the molasses and sugar would be made into rum for the next round of trade.

England Against France

Throughout the 1600s and 1700s, England and France were frequently at war in Europe. These wars spilled over into North America, pitting the English colonists against the French. But war in Europe was not the only source of conflict in North America—the English and French settlers also fought over control of the fur trade, over land, and over fishing grounds in the North Atlantic Ocean. In addition, the French fought to keep the English confined to a narrow coastal strip, and the English fought to break the barrier that the French in Canada and Louisiana were trying to build around them.

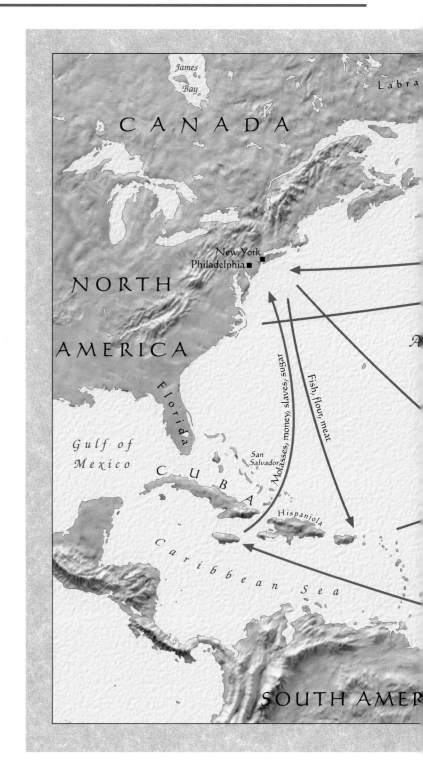

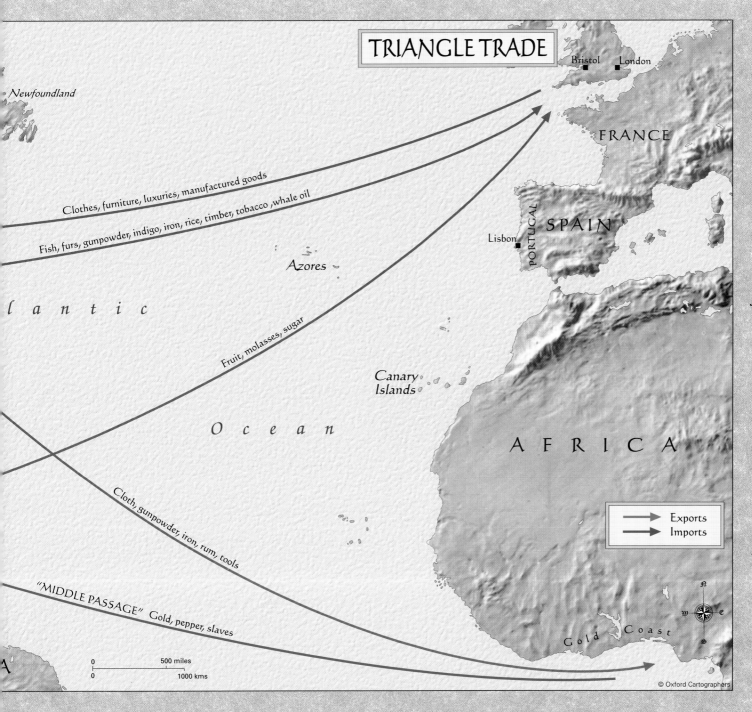

TRIANGLE TRADE

Newfoundland

Bristol · London

FRANCE

SPAIN

PORTUGAL

Lisbon

Clothes, furniture, luxuries, manufactured goods

Fish, furs, gunpowder, indigo, iron, rice, timber, tobacco, whale oil

Azores

A t l a n t i c

Fruit, molasses, sugar

Canary Islands

O c e a n

A F R I C A

Cloth, gunpowder, iron, rum, tools

"MIDDLE PASSAGE" *Gold, pepper, slaves*

Gold Coast

| | Exports |
| | Imports |

0 — 500 miles
0 — 1000 kms

© Oxford Cartographers

The English colonies in North America and the Caribbean became part of a network of exchange that some modern historians call the "Triangle Trade" because of the patterns it forms on a map: one triangle connecting England, the Caribbean, and New England and another connecting Africa, the Caribbean, and New England. Individual ships did not sail completely around one of these triangles, however. Most captains, crews, and vessels worked one leg of the triangle only.

The French and Indian War was fought across northeastern North America. At first the war went well for the French, who defeated a British force at Fort Duquesne in the Ohio River Valley. But the British later captured that fort, as well as a major French fortress at Louisbourg. They also won several battles against French forces in the Caribbean. Their crowning victory, however, was the capture of Quebec. The city's fall gave the British control of Canada.

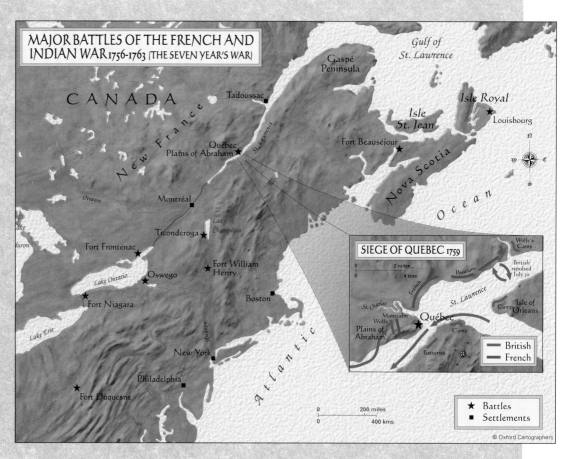

MAJOR BATTLES OF THE FRENCH AND INDIAN WAR 1756-1763 (THE SEVEN YEAR'S WAR)

SIEGE OF QUEBEC 1759

★ Battles
■ Settlements

© Oxford Cartographers

European colonists were not the only combatants in these conflicts. Indian allies on both sides were also drawn into the fighting. Tension built as a series of wars erupted: King William's War (1689-1697), Queen Anne's War (1702-1713), and King George's War (1744-1748). Each ended in a peace that did not last.

The final conflict came in 1756, when the nations of Europe entered the Seven Years' War. In North America it was known as the French and Indian War, and it gave a young Virginia planter named George Washington his first military experience, fighting the French and their Indian allies along the Ohio River. An English colonial army captured New France. Then, near the French fort of Detroit, English forces smashed an alliance of Indians led by an Ottawa chief named Pontiac. But this long war ended not in North America but at a conference table in Europe, where France and

Great Britain signed a peace treaty in 1763. The treaty left Great Britain in control of Canada and France's former territory east of the Mississippi. Little more than 150 years after planting their first settlement, the British were the rulers of eastern North America.

THE FALL OF QUEBEC

French officers gather in dismay around their fallen leader, the Marquis de Montcalm, who received a fatal wound in the fighting on the Plains of Abraham outside Quebec. The French lost not only that battle but their entire North American colony to the British.

The French scored more victories than the British in the first four years of the French and Indian War. In 1759, however, Britain boldly decided to launch a direct attack on Quebec, the French colony in Canada and the capital of New France. A young British general named James Wolfe led 8,000 men against Quebec, which was perched on a high cliff above the St. Lawrence River. The French fired down upon the attackers, preventing them from climbing the cliff. For weeks, Wolfe and his army bombarded Quebec from a distance, but they made little progress toward capturing the city.

Then Wolfe learned from a scout about a path on another part of the cliff which the French thought impassable. At night, Wolfe led a force of eighteen hundred troops up the rocky cliff. When the sun rose, the French were shocked to see British troops lined up on a field called the Plains of Abraham, right outside the fortress of Quebec. The French and British armies clashed on that field, and the British won the day, although both Wolfe and the French commander died. The capture of Quebec gave Britain control of New France. It was the biggest turning-point of the French and Indian War.

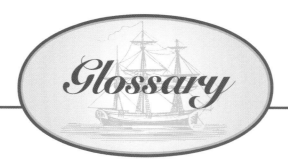

Glossary

alliance: A relationship in which two parties agree to defend each other from their enemies.

colony: A territory outside the borders of a state but claimed or controlled by that state.

debtor: Someone who owes money.

epidemic: An outbreak of disease over a wide area, affecting many people.

immigrant: A person who arrives in a new country.

indigo: A plant that produces a vivid blue dye.

missionary: Someone who works to convert other people to his or her religion.

molasses: A syrup made from sugarcane.

monk: A member of a religious brotherhood or order.

pelt: The skin of an animal, with the fur still on it.

Pilgrims: English Protestants who wanted to separate themselves from the Church of England.

Puritans: English Protestants who wanted to reform or purify the Church of England.

rum: A liquor made from sugarcane.

Map List

ABOUT THE HISTORICAL MAPS

The historical maps used in this book are primary source documents found in The Library of Congress Map Division. You will find these maps on pages 9, 10, 14, 17, 25, 35, 36, and 37.

Chronology

1598	Juan de Oñate founds Spain's first colony in New Mexico.
1603	Samuel de Champlain starts a French colony in Canada. Five years later he starts a second French-Canadian settlement at Quebec.
1607	England establishes its first successful American colony at Jamestown.
1619	The first black slaves in North America arrive in Virginia.
1620	The Pilgrims land at Plymouth.
1664	The English take over the Dutch colony of New Netherland and rename it New York.
1675-1676	The Indians of New England try to drive out white settlers in King Philip's War.
1681	Quaker William Penn of England receives royal permission to found the Pennsylvania colony.
1699	The first French colony in Louisiana takes root.
1701	The French establish a fort at Detroit.
1702-1713	French and English colonies in North America are caught up in the War of the Spanish succession, called Queen Anne's War in the colonies.
1741	Russian explorers reach Alaska.
1756-1763	The Seven Years' War, also called the French and Indian War, leaves Great Britain in control of Canada.
1769	Junípero Serra founds Spain's first mission in California.
1780s	Russian fur traders begin occupying the Alaskan coast.

Further Reading

Barrett, Tracy. *Growing Up in Colonial America.* Brookfield, CT: Millbrook Press, 1995.

Collier, Christopher and James L. Collier. *The French and Indian War.* Tarrytown, NY: Benchmark Books, 1998.

Egger-Boovet, Howard and Marlene Smith-Barazini. *US Kids History: Book of the American Colonies.* Boston, MA: Little, Brown, 1996.

Fisher, Margaret. *Colonial America.* Grand Rapids, MI: Gateway Books, 1988.

Fradin, Dennis. *The Thirteen Colonies.* Chicago, IL: Children's Press, 1988.

Hakin, Joy. *Making Thirteen Colonies.* New York: Oxford University Press, 1993.

Howarth, Sarah. *Colonial People.* Brookfield, CT: Millbrook Press, 1994.

Kalman, Bobbie. *Colonial Life.* New York: Crabtree Books, 1992.

Kalman, Bobbie. *Spanish Missions.* New York: Crabtree Books, 1997.

Morgan, Ted. *Wilderness at Dawn: The Settling of the North American Continent.* New York: Simon and Schuster, 1994.

Reische, Diana. *Founding the American Colonies.* New York: Franklin Watts, 1989.

Smith, Carter, editor. *Battles in a New Land: A Sourcebook on Colonial America.* Brookfield, CT: Millbrook Press, 1991.

Washburne, Carolyn K. *A Multicultural Portrait of Colonial Life.* Tarrytown, NY: Marshall Cavendish, 1994.

WEBSITES

The Library of Congress Geography and Maps: An Illustrated Guide
www.loc.gov/rr/geogmap/guide

Map History
www.maphist.nl

Map Societies
www.csuohio.edu/CUT/MapSoc/Name_indx.htm

ABOUT THE AUTHOR

Rebecca Stefoff is the author of numerous books for children and young adults, including a number of works on American history. She has written biographies of twelve American presidents as well as several books on the exploration and settling of North America. Stefoff makes her home in Portland, Oregon.

Index

Entries are filed letter-by-letter. Page numbers for illustrations and maps are in boldface.